Thomas and Petra Berger

The Easter Craft Book

Floris Books

Translated by Polly Lawson
Illustrations by Ronald Heuninck
Photographs by Wim Steenkamp and Thomas Berger

First published in Dutch under the title *Paasversieringen*
by Christofoor Publishers in 1993
First published in English in 1993 by Floris Books

British Library CIP Data available

ISBN 0-86315-161-2

Printed in the Netherlands

The Easter Craft Book

Contents

Foreword

After the long darkness of the winter months, the days are growing lighter and we notice a stirring of something fresh and new in Nature. The last remnants of snow slowly disappear and the buds on trees and bushes begin to swell. Here and there the first shoots appear out of the ground.

In her picture-book *The Story of the Root Children* Sibylle von Olfers tells in a most attractive way how the root-children wake from their sleep with Mother Earth and come up from the earth as flower-children.

This burgeoning of Nature is the harbinger of Easter, the festival of the resurrection. It is a festival which, in one form or another, dates from long before the coming of Christianity. In Greek mythology Persephone, the daughter of Demeter Goddess of the earth, has to live for one half of the year in the underworld and is allowed to spend the other half on earth. As soon as Persephone sets one foot upon the earth, Nature begins to bud forth. In the symbols of the Easter festival we find a number of elements which have to do with the awakening of Nature, the egg being the best known motif, but there are also other symbols such as the bread-forms with their beautiful plaited designs.

The implications of the Easter story, the Crucifixion and Resurrection, are much too difficult for little children to grasp. For them it is enough if we place before them the festival of new life in Nature, with its symbols of eggs, chicks and lambs, and indeed also the Easter hare, for in Germanic mythology it was the hare who brought the new seeds of life — the eggs — to the earth. Again the symbol of the hare as a creature which sacrifices himself for others is very ancient and can also be found in a number of fairy-tales.

As spring merges into early summer, Christianity celebrates the festivals of Ascension and Whitsun. Both festivals are related to the sky and the air and the way living creatures open themselves to them. Symbols of this season are winged creatures (birds and butterflies) and the unfolding of flowers.

In presenting the many ideas for activities in this book, the authors hope very much that readers will be encouraged to work with their children, not only copying the examples shown but eventually also producing their own variations and ideas.

1 Spring

Mother Earth and the flower-children in coloured wool

Materials
Pipe-cleaners
Unspun sheeps' wool
'Fairy-tale wool' (clean, unspun, coloured, carded wool)

Method
Take four pipe-cleaners and make the head, arms and the upper body of Mother Earth or of one of the flower-children. First make the arms by folding two of the pipe-cleaners in half and twisting them together as shown in Figures 1a and 1b. Then to make the head and upper body, take a third pipe-cleaner and twist it round the arms (Figure 1c). Twist a fourth pipe-cleaner round the head and upper body to strengthen the bond (Figure 1d).

Tease out the unspun sheeps' wool until it is very thin and twist it as tightly as possible round the arms. Keep on doing this until the arms have acquired the desired thickness. If necessary they can be made even thicker later on.

Now begin winding wool round the head. Begin by taking as thin tufts as possible and ensure that the head becomes round. Make the head bigger than the length of the pipe-cleaner, as in Figure 1e.

Unwashed sheeps' wool has the advantage that the greasy wool binds together as it is wound round. If you do not have any wind a thread over the wool from time to time to keep it firmly in place.

Wind on to the lower body in the same way.

Use coloured fairy-tale wool to dress the doll. Tease out this wool also as thinly as possible and wind it over the sheeps' wool. Keep on doing this layer by layer until you can no longer see the foundation and the doll has acquired the desired colour (Figure 2).

Display the dolls in a safe place in the living-room. They are delicate and if you let children play with them too much the coloured fairy-tale wool will soon come away.

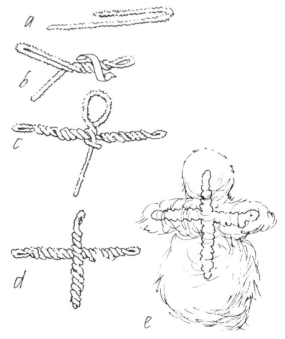

Figure 1.   Figure 2. >

Flower-children made from felt

Materials
White or pink knitted cotton
Unspun sheeps' wool
Carded sheeps' wool or 'fairy-tale' wool
Pieces of felt in various colours

General instructions

For the head take a piece of knitted cotton 3" x 3" (8 x 8 cm). Make a little ball of the unspun wool about ¾" (2 cm) diameter and place it in the centre of the piece of knitted cotton. Fold the knitted cotton round the ball of wool and tie it up round the neck (Figures 3a and 3b).

To make the body of the flower children you need a tube of felt. Take a rectangle of felt and sew two sides together as shown in Figure 3c.

(The length and width of the body is different for each kind of flower-child.) Gather in one of the open ends to make the neck. Stuff the loose material of the head into the gathered end of the tube, and sew neck and tube-body together (Figure 3d).

The doll will now stand as it is, but you can fill the tube with unspun wool and insert in the bottom a round piece of felt of the same colour as the tube, and sew it up.

This completes the basic form of all the flower-children. Now follow the details according to the kind of flower.

The crocus
For the body take a piece of felt 2¼" x 2¼" (6 x 6 cm). For the collar take a piece of light purple felt 4" x 1½" (10 x 3.5 cm) and cut it out in the form shown in Figure 5a. Gather in

Figure 3.

10

Figure 4.

the upper edge and sew the collar round the neck.

Do the same with the crocus' cap which can be of a darker purple. Gather in the felt a little at the place indicated so that the cap sits well on the head. Now first give the flower-child some hair in a colour matching the cap (for example with fairy-tale wool), before securing the cap on to the head with a few stitches and then stitch the top edge of opposite pairs of petals together.

The snowdrop

The snowdrop's body is 2¼" (6 cm) high and 2¾" (7 cm) wide. Cut out the light green collar (Figure 6a), pucker it and sew it on to the body.

The snowdrop's cap consists of three separate white petals (Figure 6b). Sew the tops of the petals on to a little stalk of light green felt (Figure 6c). First give the flower-child's head some hair of white wool before sewing on the cap with a few stitches.

The tulip

The tulip's body is 2¼" (5.5 cm) high and 4" (10 cm) wide. Cut out the red collar (Figure 7a), pucker it and sew it on to the body.

The tulip-child has a cap made of six separate red petals (Figure 7b). Sew the first two petals to the side of the head. Gather in the remaining four petals below before sewing them on to the head overlapping each other as in Figure 7c. Give the tulip pink hair.

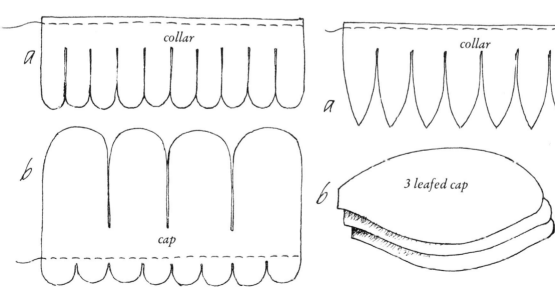

collar

a

b

cap

Figure 5.

collar

a

b

3 leafed cap

c

stalk

Figure 6.

The daffodil

The body of the daffodil is about 2″ (5 cm) high and 4″ (10 cm) wide. Cut out the yellow collar (Figure 8a), pucker it and sew it on to the body.

The daffodil' cap has two parts. First sew the puckered yellow petal wreath (Figure 8b) on to the head. Then cut out a round piece from the dark yellow felt to make the heart of the flower. Cut into the disc in two places and sew it up as in Figure 8c so that it bulges out. Sew the heart on to the crown of the head.

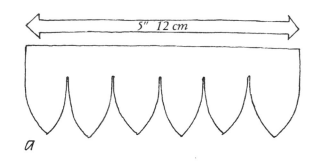

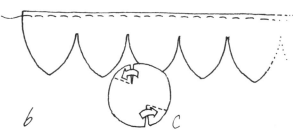

a

b

c

Figure 8.

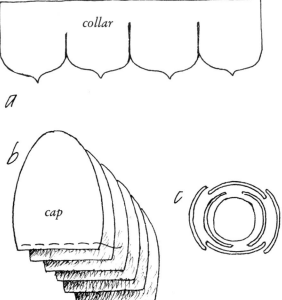

collar

a

b

cap

c

Figure 7.

Simple variation for the flower-children

You can buy little dolls of natural wood which have just a head and body. They come in various sizes. You can dress these wooden dolls quite simply by sticking bits of felt on to them.

A picture made of fairy-tale wool

Materials
A piece of cambric or other roughly woven
    fabric
Fairy-tale wool

Method
Fairy-tale wool is fine carded sheeps' wool
which is obtainable in packets in many different colours. The wool will stick by itself on to
a rough backing such as cambric or ribbed
velvet. First select a suitable colour of cambric
as backing, depending on the colour of the
wool which you are going to use. You can
obtain cambric in many colours.

Hem round the edges of the cambric and lay
the cloth on to a table, on a board or
soft-board, or secure it straight on to the wall.

Tease out the fairy-tale wool thinly, shape
the wool and press it on to the backing. The
thicker the fairy-tale wool the more intense the
colours will be (see Figure 9). You can always
refashion part of the picture as it is easy to
remove the wool from the backing. This is
what makes fairy-tale wool so easy to use —
you can always change the picture, for in-
stance, with the seasons. If however you do
not intend to change the picture or if you wish
to make a gift of the picture you can secure the
tufts of fairy-tale wool with a few thread
stitches.

Figure 9.

Transparency made of modelling wax

Materials
A pane of glass or perspex
Blocks of modelling wax in various colours
Strips of decorating wax in various colours
A hot-water bottle

Method
This transparency is made on glass or perspex.
Perspex has the advantage that it is a light-
weight substance and that you can hang up
the transparency immediately, simply drilling
small holes in the corners. With glass you will

13

Figure 10.

generally have to give it a lead frame with a hook so that it can be hung up.

You can of course create a transparency freely, but if you have not had much practice it is better to first make a sketch on paper. Do not let the drawing become too intricate. If the sketch is to full size you can stick it to the back of the pane.

Stockmar modelling wax is a coloured transparent wax which softens when kneaded gently; the softened wax is then easy to shape and can be pressed straight on to the pane. Stockmar decorating wax comes in thin strips and can be applied without further ado.

Making a transparency with modelling wax requires time and patience. One advantage is that you have time to observe what shapes are emerging, and can vary the picture according-ly, despite the sketch.

Take small pieces of wax because they are quicker to soften and you can cover large areas more easily.

As soon as you put the wax on to the glass or perspex it immediately cools down and be-comes hard, making it difficult to spread into a thin transparent layer. You may find it helpful to keep the glas or perspex warm by laying it on a hot-water bottle. Apply the wax thinly as you can always apply a second layer or press the wax together to obtain a darker colour. From time to time hold up the pane to the window to see how it will look where it will eventually be hung.

Palm Sunday branches

Materials
Some branches
Crêpe-paper
Green sprigs of box (optional)
Button-thread or thin wire or florist's wire
Cane
A cock made of dough and/or paper
Dried fruits: raisins, dried apples, dried
    apricots

The procession with Palm Sunday branches is a very ancient custom in memory of Christ's entry into Jerusalem, when the people took branches from the trees and laid them on his pathway.

Figure 11.

In the past in Europe each region had its own model of Palm Sunday branch.

Here we shall give two basic forms: the branch with a round hoop, and the branch in the form of a cross.

This Palm Sunday branch in the form of the cross symbolises the Crucifixion. This symbol can be difficult for little children to understand. For them a Palm Sunday branch with a hoop is more suitable as a sign of approaching spring, the circle being a symbol of the sun and the light.

A Palm Sunday branch with a round hoop
In the Palm Sunday branch shown in Figure 11 the stick is wrapped in light green crêpe-paper and decorated with dark green crêpe-paper. Make sure that the Palm Sunday branch is not too heavy. For little children do not make the stick longer than the child's stretched arm's length.

Make the hoop with cane. Form a loop about 12"–15" (30–40 cm) in diameter at and then tie them firmly.

Let the children help with making and decorating the Palm Sunday sticks.

Decorate the hoop with streamers of crêpe-paper and dried fruits. Finally bind the hoop to the stock with strong twine or thin wire, and put the cock in its place on top.

The Palm Sunday branch in the form of a cross
Find two suitable branches with the horizontal branch half the length of the vertical. Notch both branches lightly where they are to cross and tie them together with thin wire or strong twine. To decorate the branch more easily you can put it in a stable vase or in a box filled with sand so that it will stand upright.

The Palm Sunday branch in Figure 12 is partially decorated with green from a box bush. (Many hedges are box, as it remains green throughout the year.) Take care when binding on the box twigs to keep them facing in the same direction because the underside and the topside of the leaves are different in colour.

Then stick coloured crêpe-paper on to the horizontal branch so that each end gets a brush of box twigs.

Figure 12.

Now hang streamers of crêpe-paper on to the horizontal branch. As shown in Figure 12 the strips of crêpe-paper (about ¾" (2 cm) wide) have been nicked on each side to allow more lively movement.

Finally you can decorate the branch with an orange into which box twigs have been inserted. Cut the top of the branch to a point so that the Palm Sunday cock can be set there.

For the baking of a dough cock see page 19.

Figure 13.

A paper Palm Sunday cock

Materials
Thin white card
Coloured pencils or crayons
Adhesive

Method
Children will soon eat the dough cock on top of the Palm Sunday branch, making it look rather bare. So get them to first make a paper cock (Figures 13 and 14). From the card cut out two cocks with good fat bellies, and cut a thin strip about ¾" (2 cm) wide.

Let the children to colour the two cocks so that one is the mirror-image of the other as they will then be stuck together.

Make a little tube from the strip of card so that it fits over the point of the branch. Stick the top edges of the cocks together and insert it between the bottom edges, and glue it in. As soon as the dough cock has disappeared the paper cock can take its place on top of the branch.

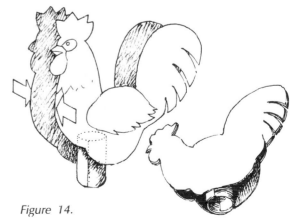

Figure 14.

17

2 Dough figures

Figures made with dough

Ingredients
about 1 lb (500 g) white or wholemeal flour or
    a mixture of both
1/2 tablespoon of yeast dissolved in
10 fl oz (300 cc) lukewarm milk (not more than
    30°C, 85°F)
1 3/4 oz (50 g) hard butter
1/2 tablespoon salt
3 tablespoons sugar
1/2 tablespoon aniseed

Figure 15.

Method
The recipe will make eight hares, or nests, or
little men, and so on.

Keep about 4 oz (100 g) of flour back and
put the rest into a bowl. Make a hole in the
middle and pour the yeast mixture into it. Stir
from the middle outwards taking in some of
the flour to make a sloppy paste.

Cut the butter up into very thin slices and lay
these on to this yeast-mixture. Sprinkle the salt,
sugar and aniseed over the butter. Put the
bowl into a plastic bag and allow the mixture
to rise to twice its volume at room temperature; this can take twenty minutes or more.

Take half of the flour which you have kept
back. Sprinkle it over the mixture and at the
same time work it into the mixture with the
salt, sugar, aniseed and the butter which in the
meantime has become soft. Empty this loose

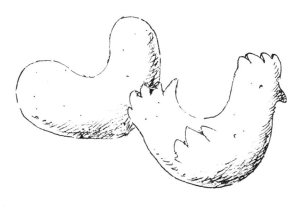

18

dough on to a board which has been sprinkled with flour and knead it (not too long) until it no longer sticks to your hand and feels firm but still soft and elastic. Knead the dough with the heel of your hand giving it a quarter turn now and again.

Put the dough back into the bowl, place in a fridge or cool place, and allow it to rise to about twice its volume. This will take three to four hours. Cold dough can be shaped better.

The forming of the risen dough is described under each separate figure. To finish off pre-heat the oven. Before baking brush the figures with loosely beaten egg or with egg-yolk loosely whisked with some milk. Bake about 20 minutes at 225°C (435°F, gas mark 7), middle rack.

A cock for the Palm Sunday branch

Make a dough according to the recipe on page 18. Divide the risen dough into eight portions and roll out each portion to a strip about 7" (18 cm) long.

Bend the strips round as you lay them on a baking tray, making the tail-piece a bit shorter than the head-piece (Figures 15 and 16).

Make sure that there is enough space between each portion to allow for rising and above all make the figures *thin;* for when they rise they will become thicker.

With a sharp pair of scissors cut twice into the dough to make the beak, pull out this piece and smooth off the cut. Then cut into both ends to make the comb and the tail and

Figure 18.

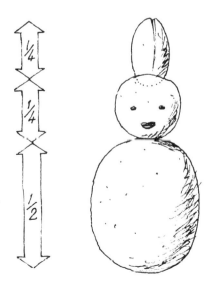

Figure 17.

19

indicate the wings with single cuts. Finally take a sharp knife and make a hole for the eye and put a raisin or currant into the hole. As shown in Figure 11 you can decorate the dough-cock with nuts or such like. Then finish off and bake as described on page 19.

An Easter hare

Make a dough according to the recipe on page 18. Divide the risen dough into 8 portions.

The Easter hare in Figures 17 and 18 is made of four balls of dough. The hare is about 4" (10 cm) high before baking.

The Easter hare in Figure 19 needs little explanation. Make two thin rolls of dough and shape them as shown in the Figure. Before baking, the hare is about 4" (10 cm) across.

Figure 19.

An Easter nest with an egg

Make a dough according to the recipe on page 18.

A nests can be either plaited with three or more strands of dough (Figure 20) or two strands can be wound round each other like a rope. Stick the ends together by using a little water.

Instead of baking the egg along with the bread-piece you can use a potato wrapped in aluminium foil. Smear the part that fits into the nest with butter. Then allow the nest to rise to about twice its volume.

After baking check whether the dough under the potato is properly baked through. If not continue baking the nest.

Only after the nest has cooled off can it be decorated and a boiled egg laid inside.

Figure 20.

Little bread men

Make a dough according to the recipe on page 18. Divide the risen dough into eight portions. Make each portion into a pear-shape and with a sharp knife cut slits to form arms and legs (Figures 21 and 22). Notch the eye-sockets and insert two raisins to make the eyes.

Take a hard-boiled egg, place it on the man's stomach and fold his arms over it. (Use only those eggs which have been coloured in a plant-dye bath otherwise the dye may come away on to the bread.)

Easter wreath made of dough

Make a dough according to the recipe on page 18. The Easter wreath in Figure 23 has a diameter of 12 inches (30 cm).

Divide the risen dough into three portions and roll these out into strips the thickness of your thumb and about 3 feet long (1 metre). Make a plait of the three strips. Lay the plait in the form of a wreath on the baking-tray and finish off the end-piece as neatly as possible. Place a greased jam-jar inside the wreath to ensure that the centre remains hollow. Cover it

Figure 22.

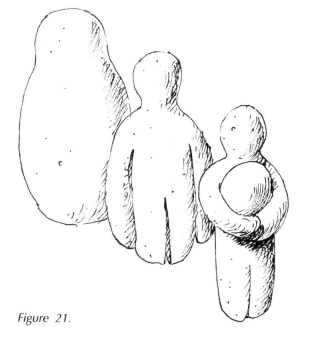

Figure 21.

all with a plastic sheet and allow to rise to twice its volume. Remove the jam-jar before baking!

Bake for about 30 minutes at 200°C (400°F, gas mark 6), bottom rack.

Before serving sprinkle the wreath with icing-sugar and place a vase with flowers in the centre.

Figure 24.

Filled chickens

Ingredients for the filling (4–6 pieces)
9 oz (250 g) eating apples, coarsely grated
1/2 oz (15 g) ground almonds or hazel-nuts
1/2 oz (15 g) finely ground dates or 3/4 oz (20 g) raisins
the grated peel of a quarter lemon or a half orange
1 or 1/2 teaspoons cinnamon
1/2 tablespoon of sugar (if apples are very sour)

Method
Make a dough according to the recipe on page 18.

Cut the dough into four to six portions and shape these into kadetjes. Cut off a good quarter from each kadetje. Roll out the remainder to make an oval and put some of the filling on to the bottom half a bit to the left. Fold the dough over and press in the sides well. Lay the filled portions on a greased baking-tray. Cut into the dough on the right side (where there is no filling) so as to make the tail. From the dough which you have kept back form a head by rolling a little ball and pressing it flat, and add a beak a comb and wings made of strips of rolled dough. Stick these to the body with loosely beaten egg. Finally make the eye with a currant (Figure 24).

Cover the baking tray loosely with a sheet of plastic and allow the dough to rise a bit in room temperature. Pre-heat the oven and bake for about 30 minutes at 200°C (400°F, gas mark 6), middle rack.

Just before serving sprinkle the chickens with icing-sugar.

23

A fruit-cake Easter hare or lamb

For this you will need a special two-part baking form (Figure 25) in the shape of a hare or lamb (to hold 1 pint, ½ litre).

Ingredients for the dough
7 oz (200 g) wholemeal
½ tablespoon yeast dissolved in
3½ fl oz (100 cc) milk
about 2 oz (50–75 g) hard butter
½ teaspoon salt
1 oz (25 g) cane sugar or syrup, dissolved in
1 yolk of an egg in half an eggshell of water
the grated peel of half a lemon
about 2 oz (60 g) sliced dates without stones

Figure 25.

Method
Put the meal into a bowl and make a hollow in the middle. Pour the yeast mixture into the hollow and stir it with some of the meal into a runny paste. Lay the butter in thin slices on top and sprinkle with the salt. Put the bowl into a plastic bag and allow it to stand at room temperature until bubbles appear in the mixture (20 minutes or longer).

Pour the egg-sugar syrup over the butter which has become soft and add the grated lemon peel. Stir and beat the whole from the middle outwards to a smooth moist dough for 5 minutes.

Mix in the dates, put the bowl back into the plastic bag and allow the dough to rise to twice its volume. At room temperature this will take at least two hours and it does not matter if it takes longer.

Take the baking form apart and grease the two halves by brushing with softened butter. Sprinkle flour over it and knock out the surplus flour. Fill the forms making sure that the ears and head are well filled before continuing and close them together. Put the form on a baking-tray into a pre-heated oven. Bake for about 30 minutes at 190°C (375°F, gas mark 5) bottom rack.

After removing from the oven leave the form closed for five minutes, then free the edges with a knife before carefully opening. Put the hare or lamb on to a grid to cool off.

Shortly before serving cut the base level so that the animal will stand and sprinkle with icing-sugar.

A Whitsun bird made of dough

Method
Make a dough according to the recipe on page 18. Divide the dough into eight portions.

Roll out each portion to a long strip and tie a knot in it. Make a few cuts into the tail.

With a knife make a hole for the eye and one for the beak. You can put a raisin in for the eye and a nut for the beak.

Figure 26.

3 Easter figures with salt-dough

The making of figures from dough was a religious custom originating from the time when the dead were given what they needed on their journey to the hereafter. Thus evidence of shaped bread has been found in Mesopotamia, Egypt and in the Roman Empire. In Greece bread-figures were offered to Demeter, the goddess of grain and plant growth. The Jews too had a long tradition of usages of shaped bread. With the coming of Christianity these ancient traditions were continued. Some of the figures which we shall make are more than a thousand years old.

The making of dough-figures is particularly suitable for Easter. The designs include plaiting, motifs connected with springtime and new life in nature, and animals playing a part in the Easter festival.

For children salt-dough is a kind of clay, but it is good to explain to children that this 'clay' is made of food, and so we must be very careful how we work with it. For this reason we should use salt-dough only for special festive occasions and not just as a substitute when we have run out of modelling clay.

Figure 27.

Making salt-dough figures with children

Ingredients for the dough
1½ cups white flour
1½ cups salt
½ cup water

Other materials
A paint-brush
Water-colours
Varnish or transparent lacquer
Thin wire (1/32″, 0.8 mm)
A pair of pliers
A rolling pin
Aluminium foil
Wooden barbecue skewers
A kitchen knife
A skimmer
A large needle

Method
Salt-dough is a mixture of white flour, salt and water. The salt enables the figures to keep their shape for a good length of time after drying. The salt content however attracts moisture. Protection against this can be given by applying a coat of varnish to the figures once they are dry.

Mix the flour and the salt well together before adding the water. Then stir the whole to a firm mass and knead it until the dough becomes elastic and no longer sticks to your hands. If it becomes too dry and granular add a very little water — often it is enough to make one hand wet. If the dough is too moist then add a very little flour.

Above all do not make more dough than necessary. To make all the figures in this chapter only three cups of flour are needed.

Salt-dough is inclined to stick to the work surface. To prevent this spread a newspaper over a board, sprinkle the paper with flour and make the figures on it. As soon as you have finished you can move all your work on the board which gives the necessary support to the brittle dough while the newspaper absorbs moisture helping thefigure dry out.

Put any dough which you do not immediately need into a bowl and cover with plastic foil to prevent it drying out. (If the dough does become too dry add a very little water.) It may be necessary to moisten the dough a bit while working: it is usually sufficient to dip a finger into water and knead the moisture into the dough.

From time to time during the work wash your hands in order to remove the fine layer of salt. Dry them well before continuing.

The salt-dough can be kept for about a week in a covered bowl in a cool place, but not in the fridge.

Drying the salt-dough figures
Before drying make a little hole in the dough to allow the figure to be hung. The figures can be either dried slowly in a warm place, or baked in an oven.

If you have plenty of time and the children are not impatient, you can dry the model in a warm place in the room (on a radiator, for example). After a day the top surface will have become nice and hard, but the bottom will perhaps still be soft and damp. Change the newspaper so that it can absorb the rest of the moisture. Turn the figure over once the top is hard enough so that the bottom can dry out too. After another day you should be able to turn the figure over again. If the figures have some thin parts which might easily break off you can support these parts with wads of paper. After about a week the dough-figure should be thoroughly dried.

A much quicker method is of course to dry the figures in the oven. It is preferable for delicately formed figures because with the slower method the surface of the dough becomes much more granular.

Another difference is the colour which the dried figures take on: the wreath in Figure 28 was dried in the air and turned perfectly white. Figures baked in the oven become light to golden brown depending on the time and temperature of baking.

No two ovens are alike. To be safe, bake a trial figure and note the results carefully. The finer details will often turn brown more quickly than the rest of the dough. If the oven is too hot the bulk of the dough may not be properly dry. The figure may even begin to swell up here and there despite the absence of leaven.

Lay the dough figures on a baking-tray in the middle of the oven and heat moderately for the first half hour (100°–150°C, 210°–300°F, gas mark 1/4–2). After that you can turn up the heat, but in general no higher than 200°C (400°F, gas mark 6). The trial batch will show what is best.

Painting the salt-dough figures
Once the figures are quite dry you can begin painting them with water-colours. Because the salt-dough immediately absorbs the wet colour you will hardly be able to remove a colour once it has been applied. To avoid mistakes work with very diluted colours. After each layer allow the figure to dry. If the colour turns out too faint another coat can be applied.

Working with very diluted colours allows the structure of the salt-dough to remain clearly visible. Children may want to work with more brilliant tints, producing a brightly coloured figure while losing the structure of the dough.

Varnishing
When the figures are thoroughly dry, whether painted or not, they need a protective coat against moisture. For this use a fixative (also available in spray cans) or apply a coating of clear varnish. Allow the figures to dry thoroughly. Store them in a dry place.

Displaying
Before drying you should have Made a little hole in the dough. Now pass a string through the hole and hang the figure up.

Another way of hanging the figure up is described for the Easter medallion on page 33.

A plaited wreath of salt-dough

Ingredients for the dough
1 ½ cups white flour
1 cup salt
1 tablespoon wallpaper paste
½ cup water

Method
Make the dough in the manner already described. The wallpaper paste makes the dough more sticky and this makes it easier to attach the decorations.

First decide on the size of the wreath. Draw a circle on the work surface (using a cup or a small saucer). Lightly sprinkle some flour on the surface. Roll out long thin strips of the

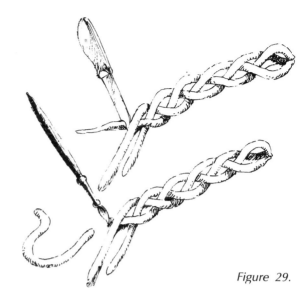

Figure 29.

Figure 28.

dough. Salt-dough is much less elastic than ordinary dough. You can get a nice even strip by flattening out the dough with the palm of your hand or with a little board. Thin strips with a diameter of about ¼" (½ cm) have the tendency to become thinner and even to break while they are being formed, so it is better to work with shorter strips and to add lengths to them from time to time.

Figure 29 shows how with a kitchen knife you can cut off the end of strips which have become too thin. Moisten the cut end with a wet brush and stick a fresh strip on to it. Use a knife or skwere to firm up the join. Make the join where it will be hidden by the next plait.

When the plait is long enough bring the two ends together, wet them with a brush and press them firmly together. Work over the join with a decoration.

29

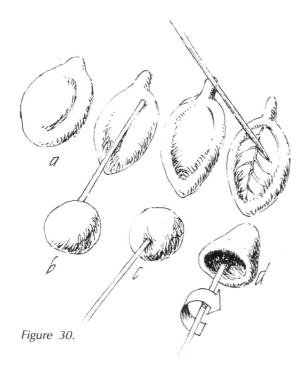

Figure 30.

Figure 30a shows how leaves can be made. Take a piece of dough and work it into the shape of a leaf by first pressing it more or less flat and then shaping with a knife and a skewer, using the sharp point to draw the veins. Sometimes the veins need to be touched up after the leaf has been stuck on. In Figure 34 the lowest leaf curls to the front and hangs free. While drying support it with a little prop of paper or aluminium foil.

Berries are very simple to make. Roll a little round ball and make a little hole with a skewer (Figures 30b and 30c). Lay the berry in place on the foundation and press it gently with the skewer.

For the flowers flatten a little piece of dough, and cut the flower shape with a knife. Pull away the waste pieces of dough and trim the edges.

To make a bell stick a skewer through a little ball of dough and then twirl the skewer round gently. The result is that the ball will open more and more as shown in Figure 30d.

Because the waste pieces are inclined to dry out quickly you should roll them together into a ball right away, put them in a bowl and cover them up.

Adding decorations

Generally make the decorations separately and stick them on to the base piece.

With a brush wet the place where the decoration is to be joined and press the decoration — a leaf, flower, ball, streamer or whatever — carefully in place. Then take a pointed kitchen knife or skewer and press the decoration carefully on to the foundation. If you use your fingers to do the pressing you run the risk of spoiling the shape of the soft dough.

The wreath in Figure 28 is decorated with a number of basic decorations which appear frequently with salt-dough figures. Once you have mastered the art of making these decorations you will find it easy to make your own.

Salt-dough for intricate figures

For the following descriptions of the Easter hare, the medallion and the Easter tree you will need a less crumbly dough, so that the figures can be more intricate.

Ingredients
½ cup water
1 cup salt
1½ cups plain white flour
1 tablespoon wallpaper paste (starch)

Method
Pour the water into a saucepan. Add the salt. Stirring all the time bring it to the boil. Add all the flour and starch in one go. Stir and work the whole well in. Allow the dough to cool.

Figure 31.

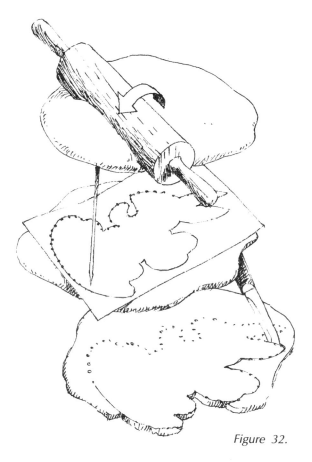

Figure 32.

An Easter hare

For more intricate figures first make a sketch on a piece of thin paper. Then take a lump of dough and with a rolling-pin roll it out nice and flat about ¼″ (5–8 mm) thick. Now lay the sketch on top of the dough and prick the outline through the paper on to the dough (Figure 32). Remove the paper and cut out the shape in the dough with a sharp knife. Remove the surplus dough and trim the edges with a knife or skewer.

Rolling the dough out will have made the surface smooth. Take care now because it is almost impossible to rectify any mistake.

The Decorations

Here also the decorations are made separately and stuck on to the foundation form: the plaiting of the basket, the twisted cord, the leaves, berries and the flower-bell.

Make the grass by pressing a lump of dough through a garlic press or through a strainer with your thumb.

An Easter medallion

Take plenty of time to make this medallion — you will be need two to three hours. The medallion in Figure 34 has a diameter of 5½" (14 cm).

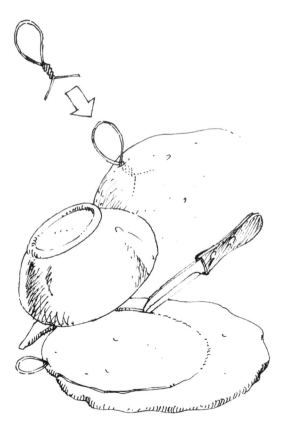

Figure 34.

Figure 33.

Figure 35.

Method

With your hand press a piece of dough flat and give it a more or less round shape.

Twist a little piece of wire to make a loop to hang the medallion up by (Figure 34). Push the twisted end into the dough (Figure 33). Roll the dough out nice and flat. Place a cup or small saucer on the dough to mark the circle of the medallion. Trim off the dough round the circumference (Figure 33).

Now make the decorations and stick them on one by one. Begin with the cord, then make the animals and the eggs. Cut out the grass from a thin strip of dough. Finally stick on the leaves and the flowers and if necessary put supports under them while they are drying or baking.

You can make the background darker if you paint a little milk on to the surface. Then put the medallion back into the oven.

An Easter tree

The custom of making a tree for Easter seems to have arisen in Greece and is probably more than a thousand years old.

Method

The Easter tree in Figure 35 is about 13½" (38 cm) high and took two days to fashion. It was made on an upside-down baking-tray sprinkled with flour. After the first day it was packed into an airtight plastic bag and put aside in a cool place.

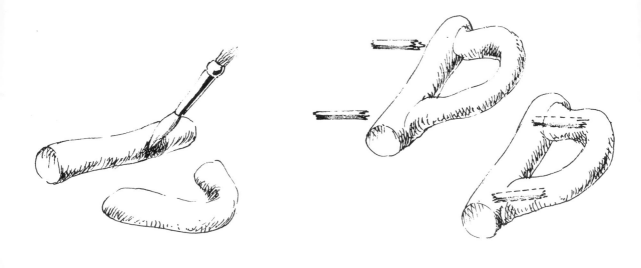

Figure 36.

First make the base. For this roll out a number of strips. Lay them together in the right shape and stick them together with a little water. If necessary use cocktail or matchsticks to pin the joins (Figure 36).

Decoration
First make the separate parts of the decoration and then stick them on to the base.

The nest
Take a potato of roughly the same size as an egg and pack it in aluminium foil. Smear the foil with butter, dust some flour over it and then make the nest round it. Replace the potato with an egg once the nest is dry.

4 A festive table

An Easter tree

Materials
Branches
Green sprigs of box
Thin wire or strong thread
12 decorated blown-out eggs

Method
Find suitable branches for this Easter tree. Figure 38 shows possible measurements. Notch the places where the branches cross and tie them securely with strong thread or wire.

Figure 37.

Decorate the tree with sprigs of box. It helps to put the tree in a stable vase or into a box with sand.

Now carefully hang the blown-out eggs on to the tree: on the highest branch hang one egg on each side, on the middle branch two eggs and on the lowest branch three eggs on each side. Leave the tree to stand in the vase or pot or fix it in a wooden base to keep it upright. Another way is to put the tree in a box with early spring flowers. The eggs in Figure 37 were coloured with plant dyes (see page 58).

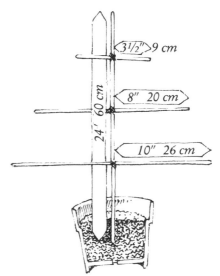

Figure 38.

Easter branches with eggs

Materials
One or more green leafy branches
Blown-out decorated eggs
Thread or very fine wire

Method
You can make a very festive Easter decoration for a room by hanging coloured blown-out eggs on a branch or two (Figure 39).

Four weeks before Easter select suitable branches with buds and put them in water in a vase in a warm room. By Easter the buds will have opened and fresh green leaves will have come out.

At Easter decorate the branches with some beautifully decorated blown-out eggs.

A box or eggshell with cress

Materials
A box filled with earth
An eggshell
A bag of cress-seed
A plastic sheet

Method
Sowing cress in a box lets children see plants sprouting in spring. Already after one to two days cress will sprout and after about a week it is ready for eating.

Moisten the earth in the box well. Spread the cress-seed evenly over the soil (and if your house is very dry cover the box with a thin plastic sheet which is removed when the seeds sprout). In the warm humid atmosphere of the box the seeds should soon sprout. Now the children can watch how the cress grows daily until a tiny leaf appears on the end of each stalk. Make sure that the soil remains damp. As a decoration for the Easter table you can also sow the cress in an eggshell.

If you remove the top of a boiled egg carefully the rest of the shell makes a little container which can be filled with earth (Figure 40).

To get a smooth round edge to the shell, first score gently round the eggshell with a fine metal-saw and then break the shell carefully.

Figure 40.

< Figure 39.

A little lamb made of butter

Materials
Butter
A wooden mould for a lamb

Method
Although the butter lamb in Figure 41 is made with a wooden mould you can of course model a lamb free-hand from a lump of butter. In that case first cut out the rough shape from the butter and then model the lamb with a knife and with the back of a teaspoon. Heating the knife or spoon may help giving the right texture.

The wooden mould consists of two parts with the shape of the lamb carved out on the inside. To ensure that the butter does not stick to the form immerse the two halves in very salty water for two to three hours beforehand. Then allow the water to drain off and fill the moulds with butter using a knife. Press the butter well down into all the crannies and smooth off the surfaces so that the two halves can be pressed together. Smooth off the bottom. Put the form into the fridge for at least one hour. Then take the two halves carefully apart and take out the ,butter lamb using a knife if necessary. If the two halves of the lamb come apart press them carefully together again.

If you are going to make a second lamb wash the two moulds well with warm water so that no butter remains in the pores of the wood. Then rinse in cold water.

Home-made egg-cups

Materials
Empty toilet paper rolls
Coloured paper
Glue

Method
Take an empty toilet roll and cut out a number of rings $3/4''$ (1.5–2 cm) wide. Stick some coloured tissue or other paper on to the rings. Alternatively stick white paper on to the rings and let the children colour them. In this way each child can make their own egg-cup for Easter (Figure 42).

Figure 41.

38

Folding an egg-cup

Materials
Square sheets of paper about 5" x 5" (12 x 12 cm)
Glue

Method
Fold a sheet in half in both directions. Open out again, turn it over, and repeat diagonally (Figure 43a).

Bring the four corners together by folding *B* and *C* simultaneously on to point *D*. Point *A* will follow on top.

Fold point *A* to the line *EF* and then fold along *EF* (Figure 43c). Turn over and repeat with point *D*.

Figure 42.

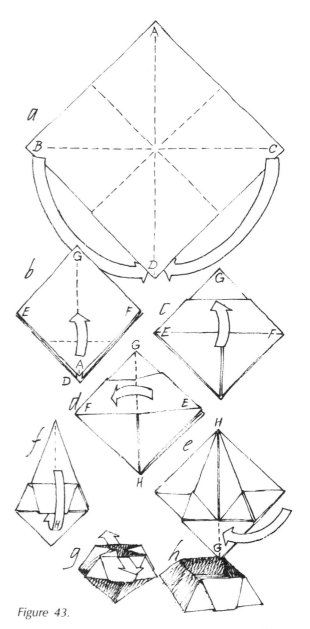

Figure 43.

Fold the top point *F* across to *E* and the lower point *E* to point *F* (Figure 43d). Turn the whole thing round 180° so that point *G* comes to the bottom.

Fold points *F* and *E* to the centre line. Repeat this for the back. Fold point *H* to the bottom and tuck the point in as shown in Figure 43f. Do the same for the back.

Now the egg-cup is almost finished. Open out the top carefully so that the point at the bottom gradually disappears and becomes the base of the egg-cup (Figure 42).

Variation

Of course you can make the folded egg-cup from coloured origami paper or from a sheet of white paper which the children have painted or coloured beforehand. In this case start with the coloured side of the sheet face up, and at the first stage, fold the coloured side into itself. The small square is white now, but the coloured side will end up on the outside.

Cutting out doilies

Materials

Coloured tissue-paper or other very thin paper
A thick needle, awl or bodkin
A pair of sharp scissors or a knife

Method

With these artistic cut-out doilies you can decorate an Easter table beautifully. See Figures 18 19, 20, 23 and 24 among others.

Select a nice colour of tissue-paper to match the tablecloth or dinner-service.

In general the starting-point is a square piece of paper folded into four as shown in Figure 44b. This folded sheet has now four layers. Now fold it once more along the diagonal *BD* in the following way: fold each of the two open sides with the points A1 and A2 to one side so that the points come to *C* (Figure 44c). This makes a concertina fold ensuring greater precision. A single fold causes small cut-out figures to be bigger on the outside than those on the inside. Figure 44d shows the folded sheet before you can begin cutting out. Figure 45 shows the cut-out doily folded and unfolded.

To obtain a symmetrical doily, use a pair of compasses to draw an arc of a circle with centre *D* from *C* in the direction of *B*. If you now cut out the folded sheets along this line then the opened sheet will show a perfect circle.

Of course you can choose a different shape (see for example the dotted line in Figure 44d).

We recommend that you practise beforehand to see what the result of a particular shape will be.

Finally unfold the sheet again and iron it flat carefully with a warm iron.

Variations

Figures 18 to 24 show different designs of doilies. The doily in figure 19 has been folded into four.

The serviette on the table in Figure 20 is made by folding a sheet into sixteen; first

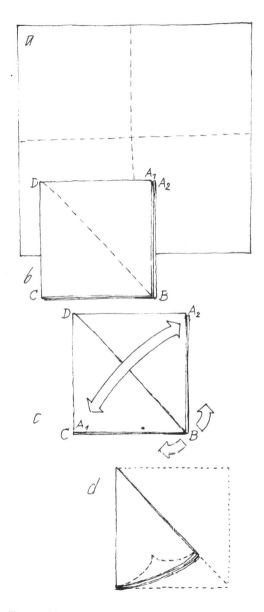

Figure 44.

sketch the design of the little flowers before cutting out.

The doily in Figure 45 has also been folded into sixteen, but was folded once more after the edges were cut out so that the design inside could also be cut out.

Figure 45.

A plaited Easter basket or box

Materials
Coloured cardboard
Glue

Method
For the base-piece cut out nine 8¾" (22 cm) strips and eleven 8" (20 cm) strips. For the sides cut out eight 9" (23 cm) strips or four 18" (46 cm) strips. Depending on the thickness of the cardboard the plaited box will have a base of about 4¾" x 4" (12 x 10 cm) and a height of 2" (5 cm) (Figure 47).

Fold each strip of the base with a fold 2" (5 cm) from each end. Lay a short strip on a long one at right angles as shown in Figure 46b and glue them together.

Figures 46c and d show how strip A2 is plaited beside A1, and B2 beside B1. In this way build up the base of the box starting in one corner and sticking each strip in one place.

Before plaiting the strips for the sides, make a fold ½" (1 cm) for the end and then fold the strips where they meet a corner. Then plait them through the upright strips of the base. The ends of these strips overlap each other by ½" (1 cm). Glue the last of the horizontal strips to all the strips *A* and *B* (Figure 47).

Finally cut out a handle from the cardboard and stick this firmly on the outside of the box.

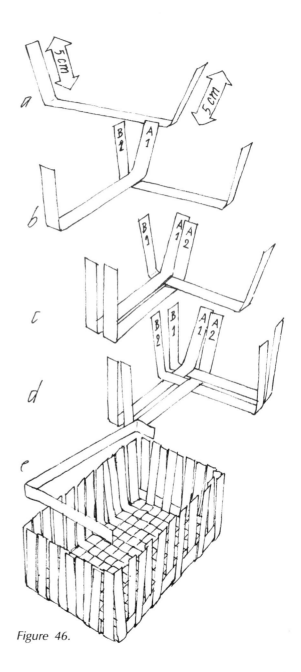

Figure 46.

Decorating candles

Easter is also a festival which can be graced with a lighted decorated candle upon the table.

Materials
A thick candle
Blocks of modelling wax in various colours
Strips of decorating wax in various colours
A thick knitting-needle or palette-knife

Method
Take a little bit of modelling wax and warm it by kneading it a little. When the wax becomes soft apply it very thinly to the candle and press it on firmly. With a thick knitting-needle or palette-knife you can work out the shape in more detail. The thin strips of decorating wax are best cut off first with a knife and can be carefully brought on to the candle and pressed on firmly. Because the wax is transparent you can lay several layers of different colours over each other.

Figure 47.

5 Working with wool and textiles

A knotted cloth hare

Materials
A soft square piece of cloth
Method
Fold the cloth over diagonally and tie a loose knot in one end. Then bring the other end through the loop of the knot to make two ears. Pull the knot a bit tighter, pull the whole thing out a bit and there you have the hare (Figures 48 and 49).

Figure 48.

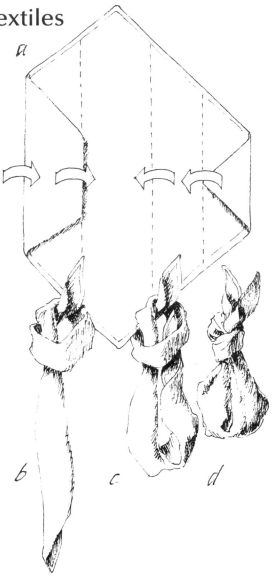

Figure 49.

Woollen chickens

Materials
Stiff cardboard
A pair of compasses
A large darning-needle
Yellow or white knitting wool or lace thread
Scraps of orange felt
Button thread

Method
Each little chick is made of two pompoms of wool, one large and one small.

Take the compasses and draw following circles on the cardboard: two small ones with a radius of 0.7" (18 mm) with a tiny circle inside of about 0.2" (5 mm) radius, and two

Figure 50.

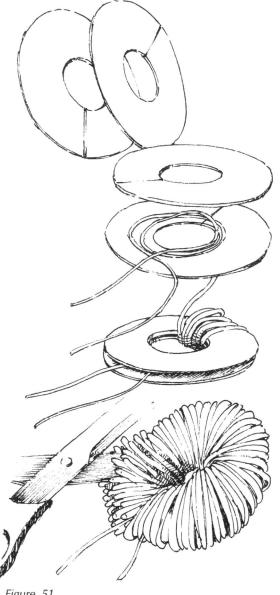

Figure 51.

with a radius of 1″ (26 mm), and a little circle with a radius of 0.3″ (17 mm) inside. Cut out the circles so that you get rings with a hole in the middle. Cut into the rings in one place (Figure 51).

To do this take a strong thread (or wool, if it is strong enough) and make it into a double loop. Lay the loop on one of the cardboard rings and lay the second ring of the same size on top of it, ensuring the cuts in the rings do not lie on top of each other. Let the ends of the loop hang down outside the rings. Wind the wool loosely (by hand or with a darning needle) round the rings until the hole in the centre is filled up.

Push a scissor blade between the two rings and cut the wool round the outside. Draw the loop which was laid between the rings tight and tie it up firmly. Do not yet cut the ends of the loop.

As the rings were cut you can now carefully remove them so that they can be used again. Trim the pompom.

Make the other pompom in the same way and tie the two together with the loose loop-threads.

Finally cut out one or two orange felt triangles and tie them to the smaller pompom for the beak (Figure 50).

Of course you can make a whole brood of chicks.

Woollen rabbits

Materials
Stiff cardboard
A pair of compasses
Brown knitting wool
Scraps of brown felt
A large darning-needle

Method
The rabbits are made in the same way as the chicks described above.

The smaller ring has a radius of 0.85″ (21 mm) and a hole of ¼″ (7 mm) radius; the larger ring has a radius of 1.4″ (35 mm) and a hole of ½″ (13 mm) radius. Tie the pompoms together, cut out two ears from some felt and

Figure 52.

sew them on to the head. For the eyes take two black beads and sew them loosely to the head.

With these rather larger rings you can also use unspun brown wool. For this card the wool in thin long wisps. These rabbits made of unspun sheep's wool have to be trimmed rather more.

A knitted hare

Materials
Knitting wool (not too thick)
Knitting-needle 3 mm (American size 2)
Unspun sheep's wool

Figure 53.

Figure 54.

Method

Knit a square, 1 plain 1 purl about 5" (12 to 14 cm). Make sure that the knitting is not too tight, as a loosely knitted piece is more easily made into a hare.

Pinch and sew the four corners together for a good 1" (3 cm); these points form the legs of the hare (Figure 54b).

Gather in the piece between the feet on one short side (the width) so that the head can be shaped there afterwards (Figure 54c).

Sew the belly as far as the hindlegs and stuff the animal tightly with unspun wool.

Tie a woollen thread tightly round the neck to make the head (Figure 54d).

Now draw the hindlegs under the body to the front and pin them. Sew up the hindmost seam, sew the legs on under the body, and remove the pins. Tuck the body in a bit so that the rump becomes nice and round. Sew up the whole thing (Figure 54e).

Make a little round tail by pinching a bit of the knitting with your fingers and winding some wool round it.

Shape up the hare, stitch the eyes and draw them together.

Finally knit the ears by casting on three stitches and knit all rows plain. The ears are to be about 1½" (4 cm) long. Sew them on to the head. The whole hare is about 3½" (9 cm) long.

A knitted chicken

Materials
Yellow wool
Knitting needles 2–2½ mm (American size 1)
Unspun sheep's wool
Red wool for the comb

Method

Cast on 16 stitches and knit a Knit plain each way so that there are ribs. Cast off.

Fold the piece over diagonally and sew up one of the sides. Sew the other side only half up. Fill the body with unspun wool and finish sewing up the side. Shape the chicken by running a thread from the point of the underside round the hen's middle. Draw in the thread lightly, and secure: this will pull the head and tail up (Figure 55).

Use a yarn of red wool with the button-hole stitch to make the comb and the gills. To make the eyes take a length of darker wool or a bead (Figure 56).

Figure 55.

Figure 56.

ribs (36 plain rows). Do not cast off but string the stitches on to the knitting yarn, pull tight and break off.

Sew up the long side to make a tube. Stuff it one third full with some unspun wool to make the head. Tie up the neck with a length of wool and shape the head so that the nose runs to a point.

For the ears use two pieces of felt. Make the pink felt piece a little smaller and sew it on to the brown felt. Fold the felt ears together at the bottom, and sew them on to the head.

Embroider the eyes or use two beads. Finally embroider the nose and give the hare a few side-whiskers.

Figure 57.

A knitted Easter hare as an egg-cosy

Materials
Brown knitting wool
Knitting-needles 3–3½ mm (American size 3)
Unspun sheep's wool
Brown and pink felt
Embroidery thread
Two beads for the eyes

Method
Cast on 20 to 28 stitches depending on the thickness of the wool. The length should go round an egg-cup comfortably. With very thin wool use double yarn. Knit a piece of about 18

A felt egg-cosy

Materials
Pieces of felt
Embroidery-thread

Method
Figure 59 shows an egg-cosy with flowers. The flowers are cut out from felt and sewn on to the background. Of course this kind of egg-cosy can be made in all sorts of different ways, also by working just with embroidery thread on the felt.

Cut out two pieces according to the pattern in Figure 58. Decorate one or both sides in your own way and sew the two pieces together.

Figure 58.

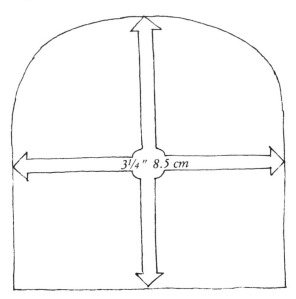

3¼" 8.5 cm

A felt hen as an egg-cosy

Materials
Yellow felt in two shades
Red felt for the comb and beak
Unspun sheep's wool
Beads for the eyes
Embroidery thread
Method
Cut out the body twice, the wings twice, the beak twice, and the comb once according to the pattern in Figure 61.

Sew the wings on to the body. Then sew the two halves of the hen's body together with the buttonhole-stitch, stitching the comb between the two parts. Finish off the bottom also with the buttonhole-stitch.

Figure 59.

Sew the two red beaks into place and fill the head with some unspun wool.

Finally sew the beads into place as eyes.

An Easter hare as a finger-puppet

Materials
Thin knitting wool
Knitting-needle 2 mm (American size 0)
Unspun sheep's wool
Two beads for the eyes
Embroidery thread
A little egg

Figure 60.

Method
Cast on 20 stitches and knit 20 rows 1 row plain 1 row purl for the body. Then knit 10 rows 1 row purl and 1 row plain (reversing the pattern) to make the head. Do not cast off but run them on to the knitting yarn. Pull the yarn tight and break off.

Sew up the long edge, so that the head is ribbed on the outside. Fill the head with unspun wool turning the front edge outwards a little to make a proper nose. Tie up the neck with a length of wool.

Figure 61.

For the ears cast on 8 stitches and knit 10 rows 1 row plain 1 row purl. On the eleventh row decrease by knitting 4 times 2 stitches together. Knit the twelfth row purl. Knit the thirteenth row twice two stitches together. Cast off. Sew up the sides and sew the ears on to the head in such a way that the seam is at the back.

For the rucksack cast on 16 stitches and knit 8 rows plain. Run the stitches on to the knitting yarn, pull the yarn tight and break off.

Sew the rucksack on to the back, securing the yarn crosswise with a few stitches to make the rucksack-straps.

Embroider a nose, give the hare some side-whiskers and sew the beads in place for eyes (Figure 62).

Finally place a small egg in the rucksack.

Figure 62.

An Easter hare as a glove-puppet

Materials
Pieces of fabric, preferably knitted cotton for the body
Pieces of pink felt for the inside of the ears and paws
Brown felt for the eyes
Unspun sheep's wool
Embroidery-thread

Method
Select a suitable piece of the material and cut out head, body and the ears each twice (Figure 64).

First sew the pink front on to the ears. Sew the sides together inside out and turn them. The bottom is thus still open.

Sew the eyes on to the separate halves of the head. Sew the halves inside out on to each other leaving the neck open. Turn the right side out.

Then embroider the pink inside of the paws on to the two pieces of the body. Sew together the two halves of the body inside-out leaving the bottom and the neck open. Turn the body right side out, and hem the bottom.

Now all the separate pieces can be sewn together. First sew the head into the neck of the body and then the ears on to the head.

Finish off the Easter hare by filling the head with some unspun wool and make a hole in the wool with your finger so that later a finger will fit in when the hare is played with. Finally give the animal an embroidered nose and side-whiskers.

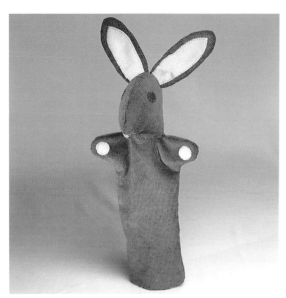

Figure 63.

A knitted Easter hare as a glove-puppet

Materials
White Angora wool
Knitting-needles 5 mm (American size 8)
Unspun sheep's wool
Two beads for the eyes

Method
For the lower body cast on 20 stitches and knit 50 rows plain. With the thick needles you will get a very loose piece of knitting.

For the arms and shoulders cast on 28 stitches. Knit 20 rows plain in all. In the tenth row cast off the 4 centre stitches and pick them up again in the eleventh row. In this way you

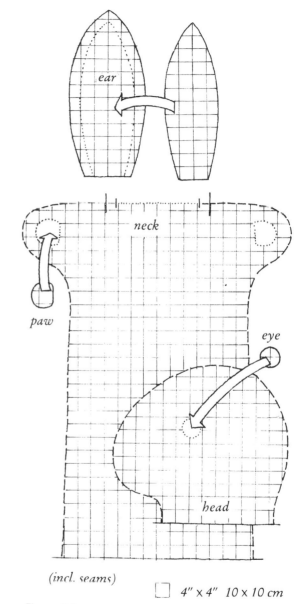

(incl. seams)

4" x 4"   10 x 10 cm

Figure 64.

will get a hole through which you can put your finger later on.

For the head cast on 20 stitches and knit 20 rows plain.

For they ears cast on 6 stitches. Knit 18 rows plain in all. In the fifteenth row knit the first 2 and the last 2 together. Again in the seventeenth row knit the first 2 and the last 2 together. In the eighteenth row knit the last 2 stitches together and cast off.

Sew the long sides of the body together with a double thread. The ribs of the body run from top to bottom (Figure 66).

Fold the piece for the arms and shoulders in two so that the ribs run horizontally.

Lay the head and shoulders to the body taking care that the arms stick out each side equally. Now sew both parts together.

Tack both ends of the arms so that they become rounded.

Sew up the piece for the head from the top, from the front and partly from the bottom in such a way that the seam is in front. Sew round the front of the nose (Figure 65).

Fill the head loosely with unspun wool and sew it on to the body, so that the opening of the shoulders and the opening of the head fit together.

Sew on the ears. Give the animal two beads for eyes, give him whiskers and embroider the nose. Finally make a tail by pushing a little ball of unspun wool into the knitting from the inside and secure it on the outside with a piece of woollen yarn.

Figure 65.

Figure 66.

54

6 Decorating Easter eggs

Decorating eggs is a custom which goes back to before the beginnings of recorded history. The egg was seen as the symbol for germinating power and new life.

Also the connection with the Easter hare is very ancient. In Germanic mythology the hare brings the new seeds of life (eggs) to the earth. The hare is an animal which has no burrow and does not live in herds. It sleeps under the open sky and leaves its young spread out in well sheltered places. In fairy tales we often find the picture of the hare rescuing other animals by sacrificing itself.

There are many ways of decorating Easter eggs. The method depends on what you want to do with the eggs. Are they going to be eaten or just used for decoration?

If they are to be eaten we can decorate boiled egg before they come on to the Easter breakfast table or are hidden in the garden. The decoration is short-lived and for once only.

For decoration a blown-out egg can be hung on an Easter tree or blossoming branch, for the whole time from Easter to Ascension. You can even keep blown-out eggs carefully for another year.

For some of the methods, for example with batik, you will have to immerse the egg in a liquid. This is not really suitable for blown-out eggs, and is better used for eggs which have been very hard boiled (half an hour or more), so that they do not spoil so quickly.

Before beginning to decorate

The quality of the eggshell can differ greatly; check therefore whether the eggshell is too thin (it can crack or break while it is being boiled or blown out) and check whether the surface is nice and smooth.

White eggs are the best for decorating but they are often hard to obtain as brown eggs are more in demand by the consumer.

Eggshells are always a bit greasy. To enable the paint or colouring to stick properly the grease should first be removed from the egg with some vinegar or washing-up liquid.

Blowing out eggs

Make a hole in the top and bottom of the egg with a pin or an egg-pricker. These holes are still too small to let you blow the egg out, so take two large round nails, one about 1/12″ (2 mm) thick and the other about 1/6″ (4 mm) thick. Sharpen the points of the nails with a file, whetstone or emery-paper to make four sharp edges. Now the nails can serve as a kind of drill. Make one of the holes in the egg just a little larger (the hole you blow through) and use the thin nail at the other end to make the hole bigger (Figure 67).

Blow the egg out over a jar (use it for scrambled eggs or omelettes), then rinse out the inside of the eggshell a little by letting some water flow in through the hole and blowing it out again, or by taking some water into your mouth and blowing it through the egg. This is to ensure that no residue is left in the shell. Make sure that no water remains in the shell to avoid problems while you are painting the egg. Figure 68 shows a very simple gadget, Blas-fix, which makes the blowing-out of eggs much easier, by only requiring one hole and no blowing.

Batik variation
When eggs have to be left for some time submerged in a bath of hot dye, make the larger hole bigger with the thicker nail. This is done by twisting the nail slowly round applying light pressure: the sharp edges cut into the egg without breaking it. The dye can now enter the eggshell and it stays submerged.

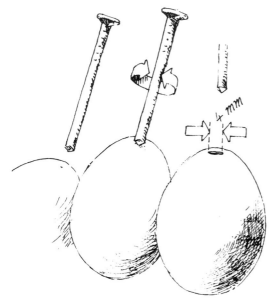

Figure 67.

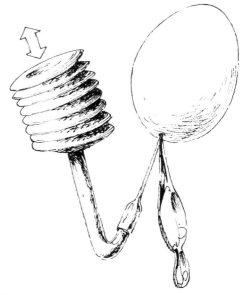

Figure 68.

Hanging up the eggs

After the egg is decorated tie the end of a length of thread firmly around the middle of half a matchstick (or wire) and poke the match with the thread through the hole in the egg. Now pull the thread carefully and the match will come to rest across the hole and will not come out any more (Figure 69).

If the egg has two slightly larger holes you can run a thin ribbon right through the egg and tie a bow in it at the bottom of the egg (Figure 69).

Now the egg can be hung up.

Eggs to be decorated by children

Materials
Coloured pencils
Wax crayons

Method
Decorating eggs with coloured pencils or wax crayons is very simple (Figure 70). For children thick crayons or block-crayons are best. Even the smallest children can take part.

Note that blown-out eggs are very fragile and can easily be squashed by children. Hard boiled eggs are more suitable for this activity.

Figure 70.

Figure 69.

Figure 71. >

Colouring eggs with plant dyes

Materials
Tea, coffee, camomile, onion skin, juice from
spinach, beetroot and so on.

Method
Everyday plant-products used in the kitchen
are suitable for dying eggs, such as tea-leaves,
coffee, camomile and onion skin, or veget-
ables like spinach and beetroot. Exotic plants
and insect-dyes such as tumeric from India,
sandalwood from Africa, or cochineal from the
West Indies will also produce very beautiful
colours. Some of these products are sold as
egg-dyes. In general they need only a short
time on the boil (see also 'Materials' on page
87).

Put the material to make the dye into a pot
of cold water and bring to a boil. Then
carefully immerse the thoroughly cleaned egg
into the boiling water. Of course white eggs
will take on better colours than brown eggs.

You will have to experiment a bit first
especially with the length of time for boiling.

Plant dyes cannot be used indefinitely. After
five or six eggs have been boiled in them the
colour begins to fade. So it is better to use a
small saucepan and make sure that the eggs
are fully immersed, or turn them over regular-
ly.

In this way you can obtain a whole range of
colours:
— light yellow: camomile flowers, marigold
   petals
— light brown: onion skin (five to ten minutes)
— dark brown: strong black tea or coffee
— red: beetroot juice is very good,
   pokeberries
— green: boiled liquid of spinach or nettles
— violet: huckleberries, grapes

In all cases the colours can be made more
intense by a dash of vinegar.

Once the eggs have dried off thoroughly after
their colour-bath they can be rubbed with a
cloth dipped in salad oil. This will give them a
soft sheen and the colour will not rub off so
easily.

The eggs on the Easter tree in Figure 37 were
coloured with plant dyes.

Painting eggs with water-colours

Materials
Paints (water-colours, poster colours or plant
   dyes)
Paint brushes
Wooden barbecue sticks or thin knitting
   needles
A piece of wire
A little modelling wax

Method
One of the difficulties of painting an egg with
water-colours (artists or poster) is how to hold
it so that you do not put your fingers on the
wet painted part, and yet being able to keep
turning the egg round as you paint. There are
several ways of overcoming this difficulty.

One simple way is to push a long wooden barbecue stick (or thin knitting needle) through both holes and secure it with a bit of modelling wax. Another way is to bend a bit of wire so that it acts as a pair of tongs with each end of the wire inserted in the holes of the egg (Figure 72).

Finally there are egg-holders on the market which hold the egg (Figure 73). The holder comes with six different water-colours made of natural substances, which are safe for young children.

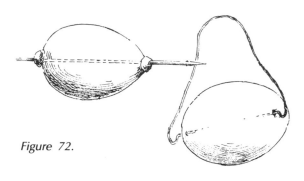

Figure 72.

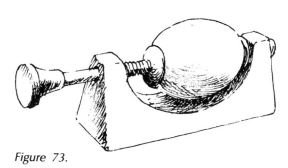

Figure 73.

You can simply paint the egg or first put it into a colour-bath to provide a background colour. Use the paint fairly thickly. If it is too thin, it will run on the round, non-porous surface of the egg.

Once the eggs are thoroughly dry apply a coat of varnish so that the colours will not subsequently run.

Decorating eggs with wax

Materials
Blocks of modelling wax in various colours
Strips of decorating wax in various colours
A sharp knife or skewer

Method
Take a small piece of modelling wax and warm it by kneading it a bit. When the wax has become soft apply it thinly to the egg pressing it on firmly. Cut out the shape with a knife or skewer.

You can pare off very thin strips of decorating wax with a knife. Apply them carefully to the egg and press on firmly. Because the wax is transparent you can apply several layers of different colours over each other (Figure 71).

Decorating eggs by scratching away the colour

Tool
A sharp craft-knife

Method
For this scratching-away technique it is important that the egg should have a strong shell. Of course you can also scratch out designs on hard-boiled eggs.

Start with a strongly coloured egg. First sketch the designs with a fine pencil. Now take a sharp craft-knife. To remove the colour completely so that the plain white eggshell becomes visible you will have to scrape away several times. By not removing all the colour you will leave a lighter shade (Figure 74).

Using a stamp on eggs

Materials
Poster paints
A raw potato
A kitchen knife

Method
By using a stamp you can keep repeating the same design so that you get a symmetrical effect. By using different colours and by turning the egg you can achieve quite delightful effects (Figure 75).

Cut a potato into several large pieces, each of them having one flat surface.
Dry the potato with kitchen paper. With a

Figure 74.

61

Figure 77.>

knife carve out a design in the flat surface and use the potato as a stamp (Figure 76).

Squeeze out some undiluted poster paint on to a flat surface, press the stamp into it and print on to the egg. Continue round the egg. If desired use different colours.

Allow the paint to dry thoroughly and coat with varnish.

Figure 75.

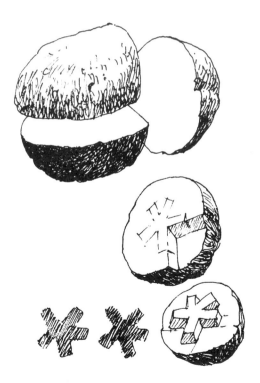

Figure 76.

Decorating eggs with trimmings and wool

Materials
Fabric trimmings
Glue
Different coloured wools
A glue-stick

Method
Figure 77 shows how you can make a very simple decoration with fabric trimmings. Just stick trimmings on to the egg with glue. Use a quick-drying glue with a fine nozzle so that not too much glue comes on to the egg. Surplus glue makes unwanted shiny patches when dry.

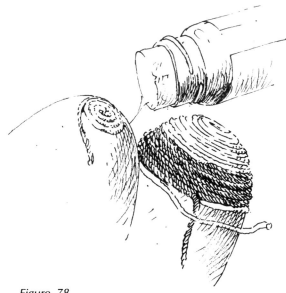

Figure 78.

Covering an egg with woollen yarn
To decorate an egg with woollen yar start by winding a solid part at the top and bottom (Figure 78). This make it possible to wind the yarn round the middle without getting gaps between the lines.

Begin by using a glue-pencil: apply a little glue to the top (or bottom) making sure that you leave the hole open. Press one end of the yarn into the glue and make a nice round loop. Press the loop well down and run the yarn carefully round the loop, applying a little glue as you go till you have gone round once or twice. Wind the yarn tightly round and round to the middle of the egg.

If you are going to use different colours, lay the new colour against the old one and run the yarn round the egg once. Pass the second colour over the yarn of the first, leaving the yarn of the first colour to hang down — which can be taken up again later. Always start the new colours at the same place (Figure 78).

To obtain a symmetrically decorated egg stick the yarns on alternately at the top and at the bottom until they meet in the middle.

Cut off the loose hanging yarns when the egg is finished and stick the cut-off ends firmly on to the egg.

Decorating eggs with dried flowers and leaves

Materials
Dried flowers or leaves
Glue

Method
At Easter time there are hardly any flowers out which can be dried. It is a good idea therefore during the previous summer to have a flower-press at hand so that you can already start making a collection of dried flowers for Easter.*

An egg is only about 2½" (6 cm) high, so for this decoration small flowers and leaves are the most suitable. Select those flowers, flower-clusters and leaves which have strong silhouette forms or which are very regular in shape. A wreath of leaves round a stem can be very effective, also a highly indented leaf can look very good on an egg. Thin petals are easily torn when being stuck on to the egg.

Stick the flowers and leaves on to white or coloured eggs with a bit of glue. After gluing press the flowers and leaves flat with your hand and hold them in position until the glue dries. In this simple way you can make an intricately decorated egg (Figure 80).

* See *The Harvest Craft Book* by Thomas Berger (Floris Books 1992).

Figure 79. ∧   ∨ *Figure 80.*

Decorating eggs with quilling

Materials
Quilling paper
Quilling-pen
Tweezers
Tube of adhesive with a fine nozzle

Method
Working with quilling paper is delicate work but it gives a lot of pleasure and the coloured rolls of paper can look very effective.

Quilling-paper work is an ancient craft using narrow strips of paper wound round the quill of a goose feather. A little slit was made in the end of the quill into which one end of the strip of paper was fitted.

For this art of decorating you need strips of paper ⅛″ (3–4 mm) wide. They are usually obtainable in lengths of 20″ (50 cm). Decide whether to take a half or a quarter length for your work.

Instead of the real quill of a goose-feather there are quilling-pens available. One end of the quilling paper is inserted in the slit of the quill and the strip is now wound round the quilling-pen. Instead of a quilling-pen you can use a cocktail-stick. If you are expert in this technique you can even use a pin, for the smaller the hole inside the better the result will be.

Once the strip has been wound right round

Figure 81.

Figure 82.

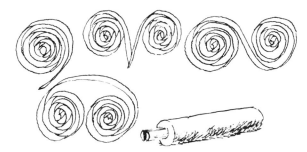

Figure 83.

the quill finish off by sticking the end down with glue. As soon as you take the roll off the quill or cocktail-stick, the strip will roll out to the stuck-on end so that you will get this particular effect.

With an open spiral it is not necessary to do the sticking. The blue spirals in Figure 82 shows these. With the little rolls in the illustration the end has been stuck down without the loop. Of course there are plenty of variations and other forms possible.

Decorating eggs with paper flowers

Materials
Tissue-paper of various colours
Very thin wire
Glue
A pair of small sharp scissors

Method
The section on flowers made of tissue-paper on page 82 describes in detail how you can make roses and other flowers out of tissue-paper.

When you are making tissue-paper flowers to decorate eggs with you must take into account the size of the egg (about 2½", 6 cm). The flowers therefore should not be bigger than about ½" (10–12 mm).

First make the separate flowers with stalks and blossoms and then arrange them so that they look nice. If you stick the flowers on to the egg one by one you can bend the blossoms, leaves and stalks a bit.

Figure 84.

Decorating eggs with straw and wood-shavings

Materials
Craft straws
Rolls of shavings
A pair of tweezers
A sharp knife of pair of scissors
Glue
A piece of zinc or perspex as a cutting board

Method
Working with straw or shavings is a delicate job. The bits are often so tiny that you need tweezers to hold them.

Wood shavings are very pliable and thin and so easy to work. Straws by contrast are much stiffer but have a shining surface.

Straws must be steeped in water for half an hour before they can be split open and ironed flat. It is better to do this part of the work the day before and to press the ironed straws in a book to prevent them from curling up again.

In Figure 86 the natural brown egg and the pink egg are decorated with wood shavings while the other two eggs are decorated with straws.

On a piece of paper draw the oval shape of an egg and make a sketch of the design which you wish to make. This entails quite a bit of experimentation.

Working with straw is more satisfying with symmetrical designs. Cut out the desired figures in their final shape and lay them out ready.

< *Figure 85.*

If you find it difficult to stick the desired shape straight on to the egg you can first trace a few faint guiding lines on the egg with a sharp blue pencil.

Now start to stick the shapes on, using the tweezers if necessary. Apply adhesive with a fine nozzle so that your work is as neat as possible.

From time to time press the bits carefully on with your hand. As the egg progresses you can see whether the design requires any more to be added or even some parts to be left bare. Begin with simple designs, and only truy more complex ones when you have built up some experience.

The pink egg in Figure 86 is plastered with squares. It is obvious that in a certain sense this was an audacious attempt, because squares and a round egg do not belong together. In such a case it is better to make the front and back the same, and fiddle the sides a bit (as can be seen on the lower edge of the picture.

Making batik eggs with flowers and plants

Materials
Dry brown onion skin
Young leaves and flowers
Old nylon stockings
Thread

Method
Around Easter time there are generally many simple little suitable flowers and plants.

Take one or more flowers or leaves, wet them and lay them on the unboiled egg. As long as they are damp they will stay in place.

69

Figure 86.

Take as big an onion skin as possible and cover the leaf and the egg with it. Then wrap the egg in a number of onion skins until you cannot see anything more of the egg. Put the whole thing into a nylon stocking and tie this up tightly round the egg so that the onion skins stay in place.

Make a bed of onion skins in a saucepan with water, and lay the egg in the nylon stocking on the bed. Fill the saucepan with water, bring to a boil, and leave it all to boil for about ten minutes. Allow the egg to cool off in the saucepan before taking it out of its wrapping. When the last onion skin and the leaves have been removed you will see that the egg has a brown colour while the shape of the leaves has been left. To give the eggs a soft sheen you can rub them lightly with salad oil.

Czech and Ukrainian batik eggs

Decorating eggs with batik is an ancient folk-art in Slav countries which is still practised today. There are significant differences in form and motif according to each country or region. The two eggs shown at the top of Figure 87 are Czech. On these eggs the main motifs are sun and flowers. The two eggs at the bottom of Figure 87 come from the Ukraine, where geometrical forms are more common.

Materials
Beeswax (thinned with paraffin if required)
A candle
A tjanting (kistka) or holder with a nail
Vinegar
A flannel cloth
Elastic bands
Batik dyes

Method
This method requires much patience and practice; in the beginning you can expect things to go wrong! It is best to start with very simple designs. Figure 89 shows a number of basic forms which of course can be developed further.

You can use both hard-boiled and blown-out eggs; the heavier boiled egg is easier to submerge in the dye-bath.

Rub the egg clean with a cloth dipped in vinegar (to remove any remains of grease). After that always hold the egg with a cloth, as any grease from your hand will prevent the egg from taking on the dye.

The simplest *batik-pen* is a round wooden stick with a nail stuck in it (Figure 88a). This was used to make the patterns in this book. You can also get a tjanting or kistka, which has a nozzle with a brass container for the liquid wax. Tjantings for cloth-batik have a much smaller nozzle (Figure 88b). By heating the container above a candle flame the wax will remain liquid. There is also a batik-pen the point of which you hold in a candle flame until it is well heated and then you dip it into a block of beeswax which produces a thin layer of liquid wax around the pen.

Finally you can apply the wax with the quill of a feather; the shape of the quill will determine the character of the design.

Heat the beeswax in a tin placed in a pan of boiling water (this prevents the wax boiling excessively). If the wax is not runny enough, thin it with a little paraffin. Use an old spoon over a candle as a wax reservoir (Figure 88c).

Applying the wax is a tricky job. You have to keep dipping the point of the nail into the liquid wax as you draw on the egg with the wax.

Aesthetically, an egg demands symmetry. Always begin the floral patterns in the middle and work your way outwards (see Figure 89 and the top egg in Figure 87). The same applies when you are making bands or festoons.

To start it can be a help to draw the design on the egg very lightly with a yellow or blue coloured pencil. Before you make lines or festoons which go right round the egg you can slip one or two elastic bands round the egg as a marker. Remember the areas covered in wax will remain white, while the uncovered areas will take on the colour.

Figure 87.

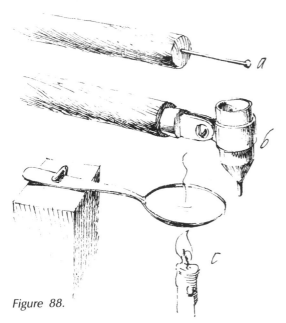

Figure 88.

Figure 89.

To make an egg with a single colour only, draw the design on the egg with the wax pen. The wax will dry almost immediately. The egg can now be immersed in the dye-bath. The dye liquid must be cold otherwise the wax will melt. Keep the egg immersed until it has acquired the right intensity of colour. When you remove the egg from the dye you will see that the wax of the design has prevented the dye from colouring the egg there, so now you have a white design on the colour background. You can now warm the egg in the oven or with a hair-dryer until the wax begins to melt. Then the wax can be wiped with paper tissues, leaving a thin protective layer on the egg. You can also rub in a little oil, and the egg is finished.

It is difficult to immerse a blown-out egg. You can run a stick or thin knitting needle through the egg (Figure 72) and pour the dye over the egg.

To do batik eggs with several colours begin with the lightest colour. With the batik-pen draw a design on the white egg and immerse the egg in the dye-bath, for example in yellow. If the wax were now to be removed you would get a white drawing on a yellow background (as described above); but now leave the wax on, and once the colour has dried make a fresh design, this time on the yellow background. Now choose a darker dye-bath, red for example. The result is a drawing in white and a drawing in yellow on a red background. Make a new design on the red background and immerse the egg in a still darker dye-bath, black for example. When the egg is removed after that, and the melting wax wiped away a design emerges on the egg in white, yellow and red on a black background.

7 Working with paper

Cutting out concertina paper

Materials
Thin card (about 150 gsm, 40 lb bond) in
  various colours
A sharp knife or a pointed pair of scissors
Glue

Method
There are many subjects suitable for this Easter
cutting: an Easter hare, a chicken or a cock,
but also simple flowers or an egg.

Figure 90.

Do not take too thick a card and do not make
too many folds because then you will not be
able to cut through the thickness.

First look at the size of the card and how
often it can be folded. If you have an even
number of panels, this will give symmetry. Fold
the card concertina fashion.

Sketch out the required shapes on a piece of
paper. Then copy this design on to the outside
of the card or trace the design with carbon

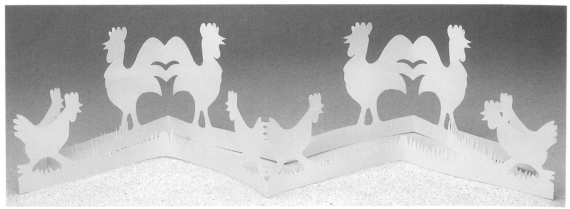

74

paper. It is important that there is enough contact between the figures at the folds otherwise the finished cut-out will fall over.

Cut out the figures with scissors or a sharp knife (Figure 90). The cut-out can still be decorated or coloured by the children.

It is also an idea to cut out two or more designs and set them up in front of each other to make a kind of story as in Figure 91 where the hen comes running up to the cock.

Easter transparencies

Materials
Coloured card
Tissue-paper
Glue
A pair of sharp scissors
A needle and thread

Method
Easter lends itself particularly for making very simple transparencies to be hung in front of the window. Spring or Easter subjects can be depicted, for example the Easter hare, a chicken or a cock. Also spring flowers are very suitable. Here we have included two transparencies in the form of an egg.

Figure 93.

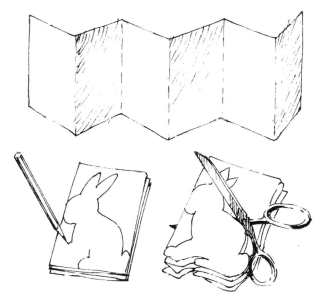

Figure 92.

Figure 94.

Take a piece of strong card and on the back draw the outside shape of the transparency as well as the design inside. Cut out the outside shape and the picture inside with a pair of sharp scissors or a sharp knife.

Once everything has been cut out take a piece of tissue-paper and stick it on to the back (that is the side of the card on which you made the drawing) of the transparency.

Finally with a needle and stout thread you can make a loop to hang the transparency up by.

An origami hen

Materials
A number of square sheets for folding of a colour of your own choice (about 4", 10 cm square)
A piece of orange or red cardboard
Glue

Method
Fold the sheet once across the diagonal so that point *B* comes on to point *C* and open it again (Figure 96a).

Now fold points *B* and *C* to the middle to the diagonal (Figure 96b) and stick them down with a tiny bit of glue.

Figure 95.

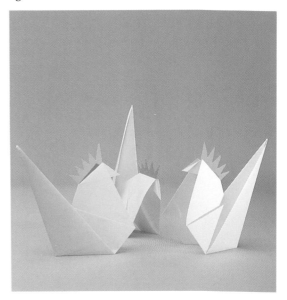

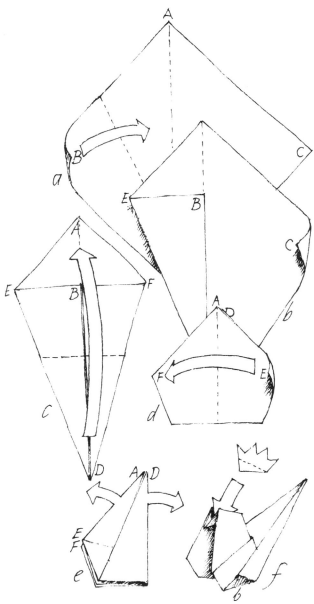

Then fold point *D* to point *A* (Figure 96c). Turn the piece round so that points *E* and *F* are interchanged and make a vertical fold through *A* so that point *E* comes on to point *F* (Figure 96d).

Draw corners *A* and *D* apart and make a new fold (Figure 96e).

Press point *A* inwards so that you make a beak as in Figure 96f. Cut out a comb from bit of cardboard and stick it in the fold which you have just made.

Now the hen can stand on the new fold. If we make fold *b* a bit smaller and fold *a* bit bigger the hen will stand on fold-line *a* and look as if she is pecking.

You can also give the hen eyes.

Sheets of different sizes will result in a flock of different-sized hens (Figure 95).

Figure 97.

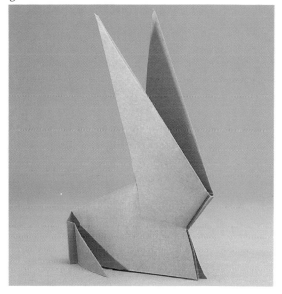

Figure 96.

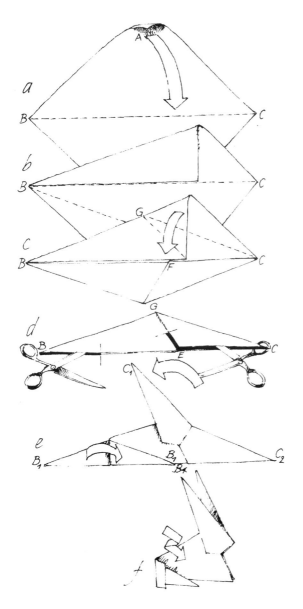

An origami hare

Materials
Sheets of colour of your own choice, size for
    example 5½″ x 5½″ (14 x 14 cm)
Glue

Method
Fold the sheet once across the diagonal so that
point A comes over point D. Open again
(Figure 98a).

Fold A and D to the middle to the diagonal
(Figure 98b) and stick them together with a tiny
bit of glue.

Fold E and F also to the diagonal and stick
them with a tiny bit of glue (Figure 98c).

Fold the piece over along the diagonal so
that points E and F come to the outside as
shown in Figure 98d. Cut into the line BC from
B a quarter of the total length BC and from C
up to point E. Then cut into the line EG about
half the distance EG.

This makes two points C and two points B.
Figure 98e shows how point C_1 is folded
upwards to make one of the two ears, while B_1
is folded forward to make one of the hindlegs.
Repeat with C_2 and B_2.

Make an extra fold at the hindlegs to
emphasise them and to enable the hare to
stand better (Figure 98f).

Then you can let the children colour the
hare with crayons.

Here too you can vary the size of the sheets.

Figure 98.

An origami swan

Materials
White sheets 4¾" x 4¾" (12 x 12 cm)
Glue

Method
Fold the sheet once across the diagonal so that point B comes over point C. Open again (Figure 100a).

Fold *B* and *C* in to the diagonal (Figure 100b).

Fold point *D* up to where points *B* and *C* come together. Fold *D* back so that the folded point is about a quarter of the fold along which it is folded (Figure 100c). Fold *E* and *F* to each

other so that the point D which has just been folded comes to the outside.

Work the point of *D* to the front, press the fold which you have thus made firmly and there is your swan finished.

Figure 99.

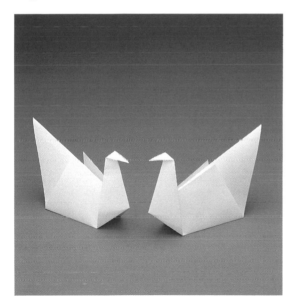

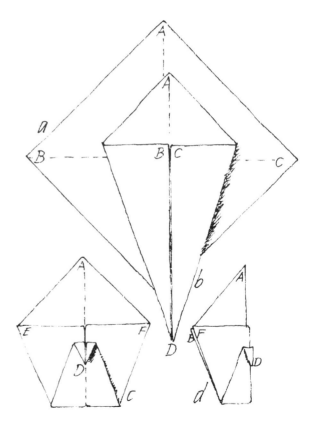

Figure 100.

Figure 101.

Little doves of cardboard and tissue-paper

Materials
Thin white card (about 145 gsm)
White tissue-paper or tracing paper
A pair of scissors with a sharp point
Thread

Method
On the cardboard first draw the head, body and tail of the dove (Figure 102) and then cut them out. Cut out or draw the eye. Make a slot in the middle of the body to take the wings.

For the wings take a piece of tissue-paper or tracing paper 4¾" x 3¼" (12 x 8 cm).

Figure 102.

Mark 12 equal divisions along the long side, and fold the paper concertina fashion twelve times. Push these folded-up strips into the slot in the dove's body. Fold the two ends upwards and stick them together with a little bit of glue (Figure 101). Insert a thread (with a needle) in the edge of the bird to hang it up by.

Figure 101 shows a mobile with twelve doves.

cover this with a blob of brown modelling wax. If necessary you can cut the ends of the wire to the right length and press a little blob of wax on to the two ends.

Finally stick the wings firmly on to the barbecue stick. Put the butterfly in a pot with flowers (Figure 103).

Tissue-paper butterflies

Materials
Sheets of tissue-paper of various colours
Wooden barbecue sticks
Poster paints
Modelling wax
Thin wire
Glue

Figure 103.

Method
For each butterfly select three different colours of tissue-paper. Cut out a sheet 3" x 3½" (8 x 9 cm) and fold it in two so that you get the size 3" x 1¾" (8 x 4.5 cm). Draw the shape of one half of the wings of a butterfly and cut this out. Repeat this with the other two sheets. Indicate with a pencil how much smaller the second set of wings must be and cut them out. Repeat with the third set of wings.

Stick the wings together in the fold with a little bit of glue. Make the 'eyes' of the butterfly out of a scrap of tissue-paper and stick them on.

Take a wooden barbecue stick and paint it. Fold a piece of thin wire in two. Twist the doubled end round the end of the skewer and

Flowers made of tissue-paper

Materials
Various colours of tissue-paper
Copper wire ($1/32$", 0.8 mm thick)
Glue
A wad of cotton-wool
Stout thread
A small pointed pair of pliers
Very thin wire ($1/64$", 0.25–0.35 mm)

Instructions for the stalk and the heart
Figure 105 shows a vase with a number of different flowers which can be made in three different ways. For all these flowers the stalk, however, is the same. For this take a piece of copper or steel wire (copper wire is more pliable), the length of which you can decide yourself, depending on the size of the vase in which the flowers are going to stand.

With the pliers make a kind of a curl at one end of the wire round which you put a piece of cotton-wool (Figure 104a). Take a square piece of tissue-paper, fold it over the curl the cotton-wool the wad and secure it underneath. The colour of the tissue-paper depends on the colour of the rest of the flower.

For flowers with stamens in their hearts take a few pieces of very thin wire about $2\frac{1}{2}$" (6–7 cm) long and tie a bead on to the end of each wire (Figure 104b). Join the stamens to each other by twisting the wires together. Attach this bundle on to the thicker wire by winding it round a loop a few times.

There are also flowers like the red rose which have no visible heart. For these take a piece of wire and bend over one end (Figure 104e). Stick a bit of tissue-paper over this end.

This will give you a better hold when it comes to winding on the flower.

When making paper flowers you can try to copy real flowers as exactly as possible, but you can also feel free to make flowers of your imagination. This is the case with the flowers in this book.

Winding-on technique
Choose a colour for the petals and cut out a strip from a sheet of tissue-paper of this colour. The length (for the height of flower) can be $1\frac{1}{2}$"–2" (4–5 cm). Now fold the long strip in two and then again and so on until you come down to the required width of the petal. This width can vary from $1\frac{1}{2}$" (4 cm) for red and pink roses to $3/4$" (2 cm) for dark yellow flowers.

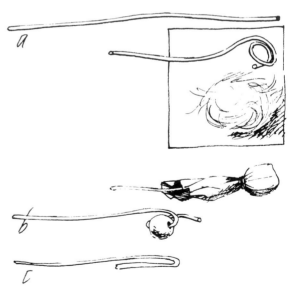

Figure 104.

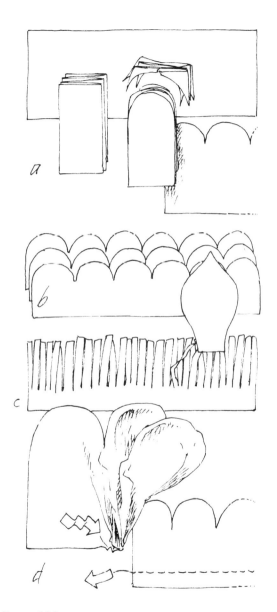

Figure 105.

Cut one end of the folded pack into a round form as shown in Figure 105a. Unfold the pack. Stick one end of the strip to the top of the stalk with a bit of glue. If you stick the strip on too low down you may find that when you come to wind on the petals, they stick too close together.

Begin by rucking the petals together to the height where the strip is stuck on and at the same time wind the strip round the wire. As you go on winding you will come progressively further down the side of the petals. Once the strip has been fully wound round the wire stick down the end. Check whether the flower is filled out enough. If not, repeat the process with a half or possibly a whole strip. Tie up the bottom of the petals with a bit of thread, after which you can finish off the stalk.

This is done by wrapping a strip of green tissue-paper round the wire. Only when the stalk has been fully wound on, stick on the leaves which have been cut out before, wrapping one end round the stalk.

Variation

It is also possible to make carnation-like flowers in which the petals consist of very small strips. For this keep on folding the cut-out strip until you have the width of a petal, but remember that your scissors must be able to cut through the thickness of the pack. Make cuts close together into one side (Figure 105c). The sticking on and the winding on is done in the same way as described above.

Method of running a thread

In this method follow the instructions already given up to Figure 105a, but first select three, four or five different or the same colours. Cut out the strips and lay them on top of each

other before you begin to fold them. In Figure 106 you can see that the flower which is sticking out above to the right has six petals. Depending on the size of the flower the petals have a width of about 1"–1½" (2–4 cm).

Lay the four or five strips on top of each other and concertina fold five or six petals. After cutting out the petals roundly all the strips will be have the same pattern.

Unfold the strips and stick them on to each other at the bottom so that they overlap (Figure 105b).

Run a thread through all the petals one third up from the bottom. With this tacking thread the strips are now tied together, so now you can cut off the bottoms up to about ¼" (5 mm) from the thread.

With a little strip of tissue-paper of the colour in question stick the top and bottom petals together to make a round cylinder (instead of sticking a strip on two petals you can of course reckon with this from the beginning and already put a little strip on one of the ends.

Pull in the threads as tightly as possible and tie up the ends. Push the stalk through it and stick the pistil on to the petals. Open out the petals nicely.

For the rest finish off the flower in the same way as with the winding-on technique.

Flowers with separate petals
After you have folded a strip of tissue-paper into a pack cut out the separate petals as shown in Figure 105c. Now stick the petals on one by one under the pistil (which has already been tied on) on to the paper there. Each successive petal comes a little bit further up to

<Figure 106.

overlap. You are free to choose the number of petals and whether they are to be of the same or of different colours.

Once the last petal has been stuck on secure them with a thread and then they will splay out by themselves. Perhaps you will have to pull out one or other petal a bit more.

The rest of the finishing off is as in the winding technique described above.

Elves made of tissue-paper

Materials
Tissue-paper of different colours
Sewing thread of different colours
Unspun wool or cotton-wool
A piece of thick wire or cane for the hoop

Method
On a sheet of blank paper draw a circle with a diameter of about 5½" (14 cm). Then draw the wings (Figure 108). Cut out the two drawings.

Lay the cut-out patterns of the elf and the wings on a sheet of tissue-paper and cut out the two shapes. Using the patterns cut out the desired number of elves.

Make a little ball of the unspun wool or cotton-wool about the size of the tip of your little finger. Lay the ball in the middle of the round piece of tissue-paper, fold one half over and make sure that the ball stays well in the middle to make the head. Tie a piece of similar coloured sewing-thread round the neck.

See which side is the best and make it the

front. If by chance the knot in the thread lands unexpectedly to the *front*, tie another knot at the back as well. Make sure that both ends of the thread are still long enough. With these ends tie the wings firmly on to the middle of the back. Pull in the threads tight so that the wings do not wobble. Cut off the ends of the threads.

Take a fresh thread of the same colour and push it through the neck of the elf with a needle so that a thread comes out on each side of the head. Tie both threads about 1½" (4 cm) above the head. Cut off one of the threads and use the other to hang the elf up by. Now the elf can be hung up properly. As soon as the elf is hung you can dress him.

Make a hoop of wire or piece of cane, stick it with tissue-paper and hang the elves on to it.

Figure 107.

Figure 108.

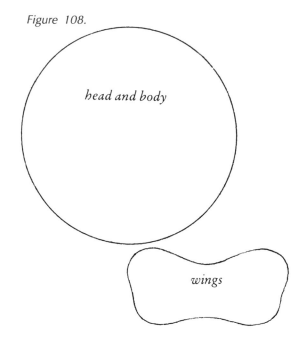

head and body

wings

86

8 Materials

Some of the materials used in this book are not so easy to find, and may take some time to locate.

Stockmar materials
Stockmar make a range of non-toxic wax products, including crayons, crayon blocks, water-colours, beeswax and paraffin wax for modelling, as well as decorating wax. These products can be obtained in some shops.

They are distributed in the United States by HearthSong, PO Box B, Sebastopol, CA 95472; in Britain by G & C Innes, 121 Bath Road, Worcester WR5 3AF; in Australia by Rudolf Steiner Book Centre, 307 Sussex Street, Sydney, NSW 2000; and in New Zealand by Ceres Enterprises, PO Box 11-336, Ellerslie, Auckland.

Blas-fix
Blas-fix is a simple appliance for blowing out eggs, consisting of a kind of drill which enables you to bore a fine hole in the egg, and bellows which enable you to blow out the egg. It is made by Johannes Zemlin of Hamburg, and distributed in the United States by HearthSong, PO Box B, Sebastopol, CA 95472; in Canada by Egon Enterprises Inc, 6705 Tomken Road, Mississauga, Ontario L5T 2J6; in Australia by Manwell Trading Company, 25 Foinaven Street, Kenmore, Qld 4069.

Dried flowers and leaves
Dried flowers and leaves have to be collected and pressed in the late spring and summer of the previous year.

Paper and Card
Tissue-paper is available in 15–20 colours.
Crêpe-paper is available in selected bright colours.
For *coloured paper* to decorate eggs with you can use origami paper.
For *thin card* you can use thick cartridge paper.
Origami paper is specially cut square paper available in different sizes.

The Harvest Craft Book

Thomas Berger

Harvest time offers a wealth of opportunities for finding treasures in nature which can be turned into beautiful decorations.

Thomas Berger shows how to make simple but charming corn dollies, straw horses, pinecone owls, leaf dragons and autumn garlands. They are all fully described and illustrated with colour photographs.

The Christmas Craft Book

Thomas Berger

Simply made decorations for home or school are an absorbing way for children to become involved in the celebration of Advent and Christmas. Over the years Thomas Berger and his family have perfected the decorations included here.

Parents, teachers and children will quickly learn to make crib figures, candles, lanterns, angels and a variety of Christmas tree decorations which are all described and fully illustrated in colour photographs.

Floris Books

The Nature Corner

M van Leeuwen and J Moeskops

Seasonal nature tables are an invaluable way of making young children aware of the changing cycle of the year. With simple materials and basic knitting and crocheting skills a series of colourful and effective tableaux can be made at home or in school for depicting the seasons and major festivals.

Instructions and diagrams are provided for making the figures and objects, along with basic hints for setting up the table and involving children in creating the whole. Each of the eleven tableaux is illustrated in full colour.

Floris Books